AF224977

Recipe: _______________________________

Serving: _______________________   Prep Time: _______________________

Cook Time: _______________________   Temperature: _______________________

Ingredients:

____

____

____

____

____

____

____

____

____

____

____

____

____

____

Methods:

____

____

____

____

____

____

____

____

____

____

____

____

____

____

Wine Pairing: _______________________________

From the Kitchen of: _______________________________

Wine Name

Winery

Region

Grapes

Vintage

Alcohol %

Appearance		☆ ☆ ☆ ☆ ☆
Aroma		☆ ☆ ☆ ☆ ☆
Body		☆ ☆ ☆ ☆ ☆
Taste		☆ ☆ ☆ ☆ ☆
Finish		☆ ☆ ☆ ☆ ☆

Pairs With

Serving Temperature

Notes

Ratings ☆ ☆ ☆ ☆ ☆

Date _________________________ **Caster** _________________________

Name of Ritual or Spell _________________________

Purpose _________________________

Participants   **Deities Invoked**

<table>
<tr><td>Waxing</td><td></td><td></td><td>Full Moon</td><td></td><td></td><td>Waning</td></tr>
</table>

Description

Ingredients and Equipment

Immediate feelings and effects

Follow Up

Manifestation Date _________________________

Results _________________________

Recipe:

Serving:

Prep Time:

Cook Time:

Temperature:

Ingredients:

Methods:

Wine Pairing:

From the Kitchen of:

Wine Name

Winery ________________ Region ________________

Grapes ________________ Vintage ________________ Alcohol % ________________

Appearance		☆ ☆ ☆ ☆ ☆
Aroma		☆ ☆ ☆ ☆ ☆
Body		☆ ☆ ☆ ☆ ☆
Taste		☆ ☆ ☆ ☆ ☆
Finish		☆ ☆ ☆ ☆ ☆

Pairs With	Serving Temperature

Notes

Ratings ☆ ☆ ☆ ☆ ☆

Date _______________________   **Caster** _______________________

Name of Ritual or Spell _______________________

Purpose _______________________

Participants   **Deities Invoked**

Waxing   Full Moon   Waning

Description

Ingredients and Equipment

Immediate feelings and effects

Follow Up

Manifestation Date _______________________

Results _______________________

Recipe:

Serving: Prep Time:

Cook Time: Temperature:

Ingredients: Methods:

Wine Pairing:

From the Kitchen of:

Wine Name

Winery _______________

Region _______________

Grapes _______________

Vintage _______________

Alcohol % _______________

Appearance		☆ ☆ ☆ ☆ ☆
Aroma		☆ ☆ ☆ ☆ ☆
Body		☆ ☆ ☆ ☆ ☆
Taste		☆ ☆ ☆ ☆ ☆
Finish		☆ ☆ ☆ ☆ ☆

Pairs With

Serving Temperature

Notes

Ratings ☆ ☆ ☆ ☆ ☆

Date _______________________   **Caster** _______________________

Name of Ritual or Spell _______________________

Purpose _______________________

Participants   **Deities Invoked**

Waxing   Full Moon   Waning

Description

Ingredients and Equipment

Immediate feelings and effects

Follow Up

Manifestation Date _______________________

Results _______________________

Recipe:

Serving:

Prep Time:

Cook Time:

Temperature:

Ingredients:

Methods:

Wine Pairing:

From the Kitchen of:

Wine Name

Winery

Region

Grapes

Vintage

Alcohol %

Appearance		☆ ☆ ☆ ☆ ☆
Aroma		☆ ☆ ☆ ☆ ☆
Body		☆ ☆ ☆ ☆ ☆
Taste		☆ ☆ ☆ ☆ ☆
Finish		☆ ☆ ☆ ☆ ☆

Pairs With

Serving Temperature

Notes

Ratings ☆ ☆ ☆ ☆ ☆

Date _______________________   **Caster** _______________________

Name of Ritual or Spell _______________________

Purpose _______________________

Participants   **Deities Invoked**

Waxing   Full Moon   Waning

Description

Ingredients and Equipment

Immediate feelings and effects

Follow Up

Manifestation Date _______________________

Results _______________________

Recipe:

Serving: Prep Time:

Cook Time: Temperature:

Ingredients: Methods:

Wine Pairing:

From the Kitchen of:

Wine Name

Winery ________________________   Region ________________________

Grapes ________________________   Vintage ________________   Alcohol % ________

Appearance		☆ ☆ ☆ ☆ ☆
Aroma		☆ ☆ ☆ ☆ ☆
Body		☆ ☆ ☆ ☆ ☆
Taste		☆ ☆ ☆ ☆ ☆
Finish		☆ ☆ ☆ ☆ ☆

Pairs With

Serving Temperature

Notes

Ratings ☆ ☆ ☆ ☆ ☆

Date _______________________ **Caster** _______________________

Name of Ritual or Spell _______________________

Purpose _______________________

Participants   **Deities Invoked**

Waxing   Full Moon   Waning

Description

Ingredients and Equipment

Immediate feelings and effects

Follow Up

Manifestation Date _______________________

Results _______________________

Recipe:

Serving:

Prep Time:

Cook Time:

Temperature:

Ingredients:

Methods:

Wine Pairing:

From the Kitchen of:

Wine Name

Winery ___________________   Region _________________________________

Grapes ___________________   Vintage ____________________   Alcohol % ____________

Appearance		☆ ☆ ☆ ☆ ☆
Aroma		☆ ☆ ☆ ☆ ☆
Body		☆ ☆ ☆ ☆ ☆
Taste		☆ ☆ ☆ ☆ ☆
Finish		☆ ☆ ☆ ☆ ☆

Pairs With

Serving Temperature

Notes

Ratings ☆ ☆ ☆ ☆ ☆

Date _________________________   **Caster** _________________________

Name of Ritual or Spell _________________________

Purpose _________________________

Participants   **Deities Invoked**

Waxing   Full Moon   Waning

Description

Ingredients and Equipment

Immediate feelings and effects

Follow Up

Manifestation Date _________________________

Results _________________________

Recipe:

Serving:

Prep Time:

Cook Time:

Temperature:

Ingredients:

Methods:

Wine Pairing:

From the Kitchen of:

Wine Name

Winery ___________

Region ___________

Grapes ___________

Vintage ___________

Alcohol % ___________

Appearance		☆ ☆ ☆ ☆ ☆
Aroma		☆ ☆ ☆ ☆ ☆
Body		☆ ☆ ☆ ☆ ☆
Taste		☆ ☆ ☆ ☆ ☆
Finish		☆ ☆ ☆ ☆ ☆

Pairs With	Serving Temperature

Notes

Ratings ☆ ☆ ☆ ☆ ☆

Date _______________________________ **Caster** _______________________________

Name of Ritual or Spell _______________________________

Purpose _______________________________

Participants   **Deities Invoked**

Waxing   Full Moon   Waning

Description

Ingredients and Equipment

Immediate feelings and effects

Follow Up

Manifestation Date _______________________________

Results _______________________________

Recipe:

Serving:

Prep Time:

Cook Time:

Temperature:

Ingredients:

Methods:

Wine Pairing:

From the Kitchen of:

Wine Name

Winery

Region

Grapes

Vintage

Alcohol %

Appearance		☆ ☆ ☆ ☆ ☆
Aroma		☆ ☆ ☆ ☆ ☆
Body		☆ ☆ ☆ ☆ ☆
Taste		☆ ☆ ☆ ☆ ☆
Finish		☆ ☆ ☆ ☆ ☆

Pairs With

Serving Temperature

Notes

Ratings ☆ ☆ ☆ ☆ ☆

Date _______________________ **Caster** _______________________

Name of Ritual or Spell _______________________

Purpose _______________________

Participants   **Deities Invoked**

Waxing   Full Moon   Waning

Description

Ingredients and Equipment

Immediate feelings and effects

Follow Up

Manifestation Date _______________________

Results _______________________

Recipe:

Serving:

Prep Time:

Cook Time:

Temperature:

Ingredients:

Methods:

Wine Pairing:

From the Kitchen of:

Wine Name

Winery ____________________   Region ____________________

Grapes ____________________   Vintage ____________________   Alcohol % ____________________

Appearance		☆ ☆ ☆ ☆ ☆
Aroma		☆ ☆ ☆ ☆ ☆
Body		☆ ☆ ☆ ☆ ☆
Taste		☆ ☆ ☆ ☆ ☆
Finish		☆ ☆ ☆ ☆ ☆

Pairs With

Serving Temperature

Notes

Ratings ☆ ☆ ☆ ☆ ☆

Date ______________________________   **Caster** ______________________________

Name of Ritual or Spell ______________________________

Purpose ______________________________

Participants   **Deities Invoked**

Waxing   Full Moon   Waning

Description

Ingredients and Equipment

Immediate feelings and effects

Follow Up

Manifestation Date ______________________________

Results ______________________________

Recipe:

Serving: Prep Time:

Cook Time: Temperature:

Ingredients: Methods:

Wine Pairing:

From the Kitchen of:

Wine Name

Winery ____________________   Region ____________________

Grapes ____________________   Vintage ____________________   Alcohol % ____________________

Appearance		☆ ☆ ☆ ☆ ☆
Aroma		☆ ☆ ☆ ☆ ☆
Body		☆ ☆ ☆ ☆ ☆
Taste		☆ ☆ ☆ ☆ ☆
Finish		☆ ☆ ☆ ☆ ☆

Pairs With	Serving Temperature

Notes

Ratings ☆ ☆ ☆ ☆ ☆

Date _____________________   **Caster** _____________________

Name of Ritual or Spell _____________________

Purpose _____________________

Participants   **Deities Invoked**

Waxing   Full Moon   Waning

Description	Ingredients and Equipment

Immediate feelings and effects

Follow Up

Manifestation Date _____________________

Results _____________________

Recipe:

Serving:

Prep Time:

Cook Time:

Temperature:

Ingredients:

Methods:

Wine Pairing:

From the Kitchen of:

Wine Name

Winery ____________________ Region ____________________

Grapes ____________________ Vintage ____________________ Alcohol % ______

Appearance		☆ ☆ ☆ ☆ ☆
Aroma		☆ ☆ ☆ ☆ ☆
Body		☆ ☆ ☆ ☆ ☆
Taste		☆ ☆ ☆ ☆ ☆
Finish		☆ ☆ ☆ ☆ ☆

Pairs With	Serving Temperature

Notes

Ratings ☆ ☆ ☆ ☆ ☆

Date ______________________________   **Caster** ______________________________

Name of Ritual or Spell ______________________________

Purpose ______________________________

Participants   **Deities Invoked**

Waxing			Full Moon		Waning	

Description

Ingredients and Equipment

Immediate feelings and effects

Follow Up

Manifestation Date ______________________________

Results ______________________________

Recipe:

Serving: Prep Time:

Cook Time: Temperature:

Ingredients: Methods:

Wine Pairing:

From the Kitchen of:

Wine Name

Winery

Region

Grapes

Vintage

Alcohol %

		Rating
Appearance		☆ ☆ ☆ ☆ ☆
Aroma		☆ ☆ ☆ ☆ ☆
Body		☆ ☆ ☆ ☆ ☆
Taste		☆ ☆ ☆ ☆ ☆
Finish		☆ ☆ ☆ ☆ ☆

Pairs With

Serving Temperature

Notes

Ratings ☆ ☆ ☆ ☆ ☆

Date _______________________   **Caster** _______________________

Name of Ritual or Spell _______________________

Purpose _______________________

Participants   **Deities Invoked**

| Waxing | | | Full Moon | | Waning | |

Description

Ingredients and Equipment

Immediate feelings and effects

Follow Up

Manifestation Date _______________________

Results _______________________

Recipe: _______________________________

Serving: ___________________   Prep Time: ___________________

Cook Time: ___________________   Temperature: ___________________

Ingredients:

____

____

____

____

____

____

____

____

____

____

Methods:

____

____

____

____

____

____

____

____

____

____

Wine Pairing: ___________________________________

From the Kitchen of: ___________________________________

Wine Name

Winery ___________________ Region ___________________

Grapes ___________________ Vintage ___________________ Alcohol % ___________________

Appearance		☆ ☆ ☆ ☆ ☆
Aroma		☆ ☆ ☆ ☆ ☆
Body		☆ ☆ ☆ ☆ ☆
Taste		☆ ☆ ☆ ☆ ☆
Finish		☆ ☆ ☆ ☆ ☆

Pairs With	Serving Temperature

Notes

Ratings ☆ ☆ ☆ ☆ ☆

Date ___________________________   **Caster** ___________________________

Name of Ritual or Spell ___________________________

Purpose ___________________________

Participants   **Deities Invoked**

Waxing   Full Moon   Waning

Description

Ingredients and Equipment

Immediate feelings and effects

Follow Up

Manifestation Date ___________________________

Results ___________________________

Recipe:

Serving: Prep Time:

Cook Time: Temperature:

Ingredients: Methods:

Wine Pairing:

From the Kitchen of:

Wine Name

Winery ___________________   Region ___________________

Grapes ___________________   Vintage ___________________   Alcohol % ___________________

Appearance		☆ ☆ ☆ ☆ ☆
Aroma		☆ ☆ ☆ ☆ ☆
Body		☆ ☆ ☆ ☆ ☆
Taste		☆ ☆ ☆ ☆ ☆
Finish		☆ ☆ ☆ ☆ ☆

Pairs With

Serving Temperature

Notes

Ratings ☆ ☆ ☆ ☆ ☆

Date _______________________   **Caster** _______________________

Name of Ritual or Spell _______________________

Purpose _______________________

Participants   **Deities Invoked**

Waxing	Full Moon	Waning

Description

Ingredients and Equipment

Immediate feelings and effects

Follow Up

Manifestation Date _______________________

Results _______________________

Recipe: ________________________

Serving: ________________   Prep Time: ________________

Cook Time: ________________   Temperature: ________________

Ingredients:

____
____
____
____
____
____
____
____
____
____
____
____

Methods:

____
____
____
____
____
____
____
____
____
____
____
____

Wine Pairing: ________________________

From the Kitchen of: ________________________

Wine Name

Winery ___________________   Region _______________________________

Grapes _______________________   Vintage _______________   Alcohol % ___________

Appearance		☆ ☆ ☆ ☆ ☆
Aroma		☆ ☆ ☆ ☆ ☆
Body		☆ ☆ ☆ ☆ ☆
Taste		☆ ☆ ☆ ☆ ☆
Finish		☆ ☆ ☆ ☆ ☆

Pairs With	Serving Temperature

Notes

Ratings ☆ ☆ ☆ ☆ ☆

Date ______________________________   **Caster** ______________________________

Name of Ritual or Spell ______________________________

Purpose ______________________________

Participants   **Deities Invoked**

Waxing   Full Moon   Waning

Description

Ingredients and Equipment

Immediate feelings and effects

Follow Up

Manifestation Date ______________________________

Results ______________________________

Recipe:

Serving: Prep Time:

Cook Time: Temperature:

Ingredients: Methods:

Wine Pairing:

From the Kitchen of:

Wine Name

Winery _______________ Region _______________

Grapes _______________ Vintage _______________ Alcohol % _______________

		Rating
Appearance		☆ ☆ ☆ ☆ ☆
Aroma		☆ ☆ ☆ ☆ ☆
Body		☆ ☆ ☆ ☆ ☆
Taste		☆ ☆ ☆ ☆ ☆
Finish		☆ ☆ ☆ ☆ ☆

Pairs With

Serving Temperature

Notes

Ratings ☆ ☆ ☆ ☆ ☆

Date _______________________________   **Caster** _______________________________

Name of Ritual or Spell _______________________________

Purpose _______________________________

Participants   **Deities Invoked**

| Waxing | | | Full Moon | | Waning | |

Description

Ingredients and Equipment

Immediate feelings and effects

Follow Up

Manifestation Date _______________________________

Results _______________________________

Recipe: _______________________

Serving: _______________   Prep Time: _______________

Cook Time: _______________   Temperature: _______________

Ingredients:

____

____

____

____

____

____

____

____

____

____

____

____

____

Methods:

____

____

____

____

____

____

____

____

____

____

____

____

____

Wine Pairing: _______________________

From the Kitchen of: _______________________

Wine Name

Winery

Region

Grapes

Vintage

Alcohol %

Appearance		☆ ☆ ☆ ☆ ☆
Aroma		☆ ☆ ☆ ☆ ☆
Body		☆ ☆ ☆ ☆ ☆
Taste		☆ ☆ ☆ ☆ ☆
Finish		☆ ☆ ☆ ☆ ☆

Pairs With

Serving Temperature

Notes

Ratings ☆ ☆ ☆ ☆ ☆

Date ______________________________   **Caster** ______________________________

Name of Ritual or Spell ______________________________

Purpose ______________________________

Participants   **Deities Invoked**

Waxing   Full Moon   Waning

Description

Ingredients and Equipment

Immediate feelings and effects

Follow Up

Manifestation Date ______________________________

Results ______________________________

Recipe: ___________________________________

Serving: ___________________   Prep Time: ___________________

Cook Time: _________________   Temperature: _________________

Ingredients:

____

____

____

____

____

____

____

____

____

____

____

____

Methods:

____

____

____

____

____

____

____

____

____

____

____

____

Wine Pairing: ______________________________

From the Kitchen of: _______________________

Wine Name

Winery

Region

Grapes

Vintage

Alcohol %

Appearance		☆ ☆ ☆ ☆ ☆
Aroma		☆ ☆ ☆ ☆ ☆
Body		☆ ☆ ☆ ☆ ☆
Taste		☆ ☆ ☆ ☆ ☆
Finish		☆ ☆ ☆ ☆ ☆

Pairs With

Serving Temperature

Notes

Ratings ☆ ☆ ☆ ☆ ☆

Date _________________________________   **Caster** _________________________________

Name of Ritual or Spell _________________________________

Purpose _________________________________

Participants   **Deities Invoked**

Waxing			Full Moon		Waning	

Description

Ingredients and Equipment

Immediate feelings and effects

Follow Up

Manifestation Date _________________________________

Results _________________________________

Recipe:

Serving: Prep Time:

Cook Time: Temperature:

Ingredients: Methods:

Wine Pairing:

From the Kitchen of:

Wine Name

Winery ________________________   Region ________________________

Grapes ________________________   Vintage ________________   Alcohol % ____________

Appearance		☆ ☆ ☆ ☆ ☆
Aroma		☆ ☆ ☆ ☆ ☆
Body		☆ ☆ ☆ ☆ ☆
Taste		☆ ☆ ☆ ☆ ☆
Finish		☆ ☆ ☆ ☆ ☆

Pairs With

Serving Temperature

Notes

Ratings ☆ ☆ ☆ ☆ ☆

Date _________________________   **Caster** _________________________

Name of Ritual or Spell _________________________

Purpose _________________________

Participants   **Deities Invoked**

Waxing   Full Moon   Waning

Description

Ingredients and Equipment

Immediate feelings and effects

Follow Up

Manifestation Date _________________________

Results _________________________

Recipe:

Serving:

Prep Time:

Cook Time:

Temperature:

Ingredients:

Methods:

Wine Pairing:

From the Kitchen of:

Wine Name

Winery ___________________   Region ___________________

Grapes ___________________   Vintage ___________________   Alcohol % ___________

		Rating
Appearance		☆ ☆ ☆ ☆ ☆
Aroma		☆ ☆ ☆ ☆ ☆
Body		☆ ☆ ☆ ☆ ☆
Taste		☆ ☆ ☆ ☆ ☆
Finish		☆ ☆ ☆ ☆ ☆

Pairs With	Serving Temperature

Notes

Ratings ☆ ☆ ☆ ☆ ☆

Date _______________________   **Caster** _______________________

Name of Ritual or Spell _______________________

Purpose _______________________

Participants   **Deities Invoked**

Waxing   Full Moon   Waning

Description

Ingredients and Equipment

Immediate feelings and effects

Follow Up

Manifestation Date _______________________

Results _______________________

Recipe: _______________________

Serving: _______________________   Prep Time: _______________________

Cook Time: _______________________   Temperature: _______________________

Ingredients:

____

____

____

____

____

____

____

____

____

____

____

____

____

Methods:

____

____

____

____

____

____

____

____

____

____

____

____

____

Wine Pairing: ____

From the Kitchen of: ____

Wine Name

Winery ___________________   Region ___________________

Grapes ___________________   Vintage ___________________   Alcohol % ___________________

Appearance		☆ ☆ ☆ ☆ ☆
Aroma		☆ ☆ ☆ ☆ ☆
Body		☆ ☆ ☆ ☆ ☆
Taste		☆ ☆ ☆ ☆ ☆
Finish		☆ ☆ ☆ ☆ ☆

Pairs With

Serving Temperature

Notes

Ratings ☆ ☆ ☆ ☆ ☆

Date _______________________   **Caster** _______________________

Name of Ritual or Spell _______________________

Purpose _______________________

Participants   **Deities Invoked**

Waxing   Full Moon   Waning

Description

Ingredients and Equipment

Immediate feelings and effects

Follow Up

Manifestation Date _______________________

Results _______________________

Recipe:

Serving: Prep Time:

Cook Time: Temperature:

Ingredients: Methods:

Wine Pairing:

From the Kitchen of:

Wine Name

Winery

Region

Grapes

Vintage

Alcohol %

Appearance		☆ ☆ ☆ ☆ ☆
Aroma		☆ ☆ ☆ ☆ ☆
Body		☆ ☆ ☆ ☆ ☆
Taste		☆ ☆ ☆ ☆ ☆
Finish		☆ ☆ ☆ ☆ ☆

Pairs With

Serving
Temperature

Notes

Ratings ☆ ☆ ☆ ☆ ☆

Date _______________________   **Caster** _______________________

Name of Ritual or Spell _______________________

Purpose _______________________

Participants   **Deities Invoked**

Waxing	Full Moon	Waning

Description

Ingredients and Equipment

Immediate feelings and effects

Follow Up

Manifestation Date _______________________

Results _______________________

Recipe:

Serving:

Prep Time:

Cook Time:

Temperature:

Ingredients:

Methods:

Wine Pairing:

From the Kitchen of:

Wine Name

Winery ___________________   Region ___________________

Grapes ___________________   Vintage ___________________   Alcohol % ___________

		Rating
Appearance		☆ ☆ ☆ ☆ ☆
Aroma		☆ ☆ ☆ ☆ ☆
Body		☆ ☆ ☆ ☆ ☆
Taste		☆ ☆ ☆ ☆ ☆
Finish		☆ ☆ ☆ ☆ ☆

Pairs With

Serving Temperature

Notes

Ratings ☆ ☆ ☆ ☆ ☆

Date _________________________________   **Caster** _________________________________

Name of Ritual or Spell _________________________________

Purpose _________________________________

Participants   **Deities Invoked**

Waxing   Full Moon   Waning

Description

Ingredients and Equipment

Immediate feelings and effects

Follow Up

Manifestation Date _________________________________

Results _________________________________

Recipe:

Serving:

Prep Time:

Cook Time:

Temperature:

Ingredients:

Methods:

Wine Pairing:

From the Kitchen of:

Wine Name

Winery ______________________   Region ______________________

Grapes ______________________   Vintage ______________________   Alcohol % ______________________

Appearance		☆ ☆ ☆ ☆ ☆
Aroma		☆ ☆ ☆ ☆ ☆
Body		☆ ☆ ☆ ☆ ☆
Taste		☆ ☆ ☆ ☆ ☆
Finish		☆ ☆ ☆ ☆ ☆

Pairs With	Serving Temperature

Notes

Ratings ☆ ☆ ☆ ☆ ☆

Date _______________________________   **Caster** _______________________________

Name of Ritual or Spell ____

Purpose ____

Participants   **Deities Invoked**

Waxing   Full Moon   Waning

Description

Ingredients and Equipment

Immediate feelings and effects

Follow Up

Manifestation Date _______________________________

Results _______________________________

Recipe: ________________________

Serving: ________________   Prep Time: ________________

Cook Time: ________________   Temperature: ________________

Ingredients:

____
____
____
____
____
____
____
____
____
____
____
____

Methods:

____
____
____
____
____
____
____
____
____
____
____
____

Wine Pairing: ________________________

From the Kitchen of: ________________________

Wine Name

Winery ___________________   Region ___________________

Grapes ___________________   Vintage ___________   Alcohol % ___________

		Rating
Appearance		☆ ☆ ☆ ☆ ☆
Aroma		☆ ☆ ☆ ☆ ☆
Body		☆ ☆ ☆ ☆ ☆
Taste		☆ ☆ ☆ ☆ ☆
Finish		☆ ☆ ☆ ☆ ☆

Pairs With

Serving Temperature

Notes

Ratings ☆ ☆ ☆ ☆ ☆

Date ______________________________   **Caster** ______________________________

Name of Ritual or Spell ______________________________

Purpose ______________________________

Participants   **Deities Invoked**

Waxing   Full Moon   Waning

Description

Ingredients and Equipment

Immediate feelings and effects

Follow Up

Manifestation Date ______________________________

Results ______________________________

Recipe:

Serving:

Prep Time:

Cook Time:

Temperature:

Ingredients:

Methods:

Wine Pairing:

From the Kitchen of:

Wine Name

Winery

Region

Grapes

Vintage

Alcohol %

Appearance		☆ ☆ ☆ ☆ ☆
Aroma		☆ ☆ ☆ ☆ ☆
Body		☆ ☆ ☆ ☆ ☆
Taste		☆ ☆ ☆ ☆ ☆
Finish		☆ ☆ ☆ ☆ ☆

Pairs With

Serving Temperature

Notes

Ratings ☆ ☆ ☆ ☆ ☆

Date ___________________________ **Caster** ___________________________

Name of Ritual or Spell ___________________________

Purpose ___________________________

Participants   **Deities Invoked**

Waxing   Full Moon   Waning

Description

Ingredients and Equipment

Immediate feelings and effects

Follow Up

Manifestation Date ___________________________

Results ___________________________

Recipe:

Serving:

Prep Time:

Cook Time:

Temperature:

Ingredients:

Methods:

Wine Pairing:

From the Kitchen of:

Wine Name

Winery

Region

Grapes

Vintage

Alcohol %

		Rating
Appearance		☆ ☆ ☆ ☆ ☆
Aroma		☆ ☆ ☆ ☆ ☆
Body		☆ ☆ ☆ ☆ ☆
Taste		☆ ☆ ☆ ☆ ☆
Finish		☆ ☆ ☆ ☆ ☆

Pairs With

Serving Temperature

Notes

Ratings ☆ ☆ ☆ ☆ ☆

Date _______________________ **Caster** _______________________

Name of Ritual or Spell _______________________

Purpose _______________________

Participants   **Deities Invoked**

Waxing   Full Moon   Waning

Description

Ingredients and Equipment

Immediate feelings and effects

Follow Up

Manifestation Date _______________________

Results _______________________

Recipe:

Serving:

Cook Time:

Prep Time:

Temperature:

Ingredients:

Methods:

Wine Pairing:

From the Kitchen of:

Wine Name

Winery ___________________   Region ___________________

Grapes ___________________   Vintage ___________________   Alcohol % ___________

Appearance		☆ ☆ ☆ ☆ ☆
Aroma		☆ ☆ ☆ ☆ ☆
Body		☆ ☆ ☆ ☆ ☆
Taste		☆ ☆ ☆ ☆ ☆
Finish		☆ ☆ ☆ ☆ ☆

Pairs With	Serving Temperature

Notes

Ratings ☆ ☆ ☆ ☆ ☆

Date ___________________________   **Caster** ___________________________

Name of Ritual or Spell ____

Purpose ____

Participants   **Deities Invoked**

Waxing   Full Moon   Waning

Description

Ingredients and Equipment

Immediate feelings and effects

Follow Up

Manifestation Date ____

Results ____

Recipe:

Serving: Prep Time:

Cook Time: Temperature:

Ingredients: Methods:

Wine Pairing:

From the Kitchen of:

Wine Name

Winery ________________________   Region ________________________

Grapes ________________________   Vintage ________________   Alcohol % ________

Appearance		☆ ☆ ☆ ☆ ☆
Aroma		☆ ☆ ☆ ☆ ☆
Body		☆ ☆ ☆ ☆ ☆
Taste		☆ ☆ ☆ ☆ ☆
Finish		☆ ☆ ☆ ☆ ☆

Pairs With

Serving Temperature

Notes

Ratings ☆ ☆ ☆ ☆ ☆

Date _______________________________   **Caster** _______________________________

Name of Ritual or Spell ____

Purpose ____

Participants   **Deities Invoked**

| Waxing | | | Full Moon | | Waning | |

Description

Ingredients and Equipment

Immediate feelings and effects

Follow Up

Manifestation Date ____

Results ____

Recipe:

Serving:

Prep Time:

Cook Time:

Temperature:

Ingredients:

Methods:

Wine Pairing:

From the Kitchen of:

Wine Name

Winery _____________ Region _____________

Grapes _____________ Vintage _____________ Alcohol % _____________

Appearance		☆ ☆ ☆ ☆ ☆
Aroma		☆ ☆ ☆ ☆ ☆
Body		☆ ☆ ☆ ☆ ☆
Taste		☆ ☆ ☆ ☆ ☆
Finish		☆ ☆ ☆ ☆ ☆

Pairs With	Serving Temperature

Notes

Ratings ☆ ☆ ☆ ☆ ☆

Date ___________________________   **Caster** ___________________________

Name of Ritual or Spell ___________________________

Purpose ___________________________

Participants   **Deities Invoked**

Waxing   Full Moon   Waning

Description

Ingredients and Equipment

Immediate feelings and effects

Follow Up

Manifestation Date ___________________________

Results ___________________________

Plant Name   **Date Planted**

Water
Requirements 🌢 🌢🌢 🌢🌢🌢   Sunlight ☀ ◐ ●

☐ Seed   ☐ Transplant

Date	Event

Notes

Outcome

Uses

Purchased at: _________________________________ Price: _____________

Plant Name   **Date Planted**

Water
Requirements   Sunlight

☐ Seed   ☐ Transplant

Date	Event

Notes

Outcome

Uses

Purchased at: _______________________________   Price: _______________

Plant Name   **Date Planted**

Water
Requirements 💧 💧💧 💧💧💧   Sunlight

☐ Seed   ☐ Transplant

Date	Event

Notes

Outcome

Uses

Purchased at: _______________________________   Price: _______________

<table>
<tr><td>Plant Name</td><td>Date Planted</td></tr>
</table>

Water Requirements

Sunlight

☐ Seed ☐ Transplant

Date	Event

Notes

Outcome

Uses

Purchased at: _______________________ Price: _______________________

Plant Name   **Date Planted**

Water
Requirements   💧   💧💧   💧💧💧   Sunlight   ☀ ☀ ●

☐ Seed   ☐ Transplant

Date	Event

Notes

Outcome

Uses

Purchased at: _______________________________   Price: _______________

| **Plant Name** | **Date Planted** |

Water
Requirements

Sunlight

☐ Seed   ☐ Transplant

Date	Event

Notes

Outcome

Uses

Purchased at: _________________________   Price: _________________________

Plant Name	**Date Planted**

Water Requirements

Sunlight

☐ Seed   ☐ Transplant

Date	Event

Notes

Outcome

Uses

Purchased at: _______________________________   Price: _______________

Plant Name	**Date Planted**

Water Requirements

Sunlight

☐ Seed   ☐ Transplant

Date	Event

Notes

Outcome

Uses

Purchased at: _________________________   Price: _____________

Plant Name   **Date Planted**

Water
Requirements 💧   💧💧   💧💧💧   Sunlight ☀ ◑ ●

☐ Seed   ☐ Transplant

Date	Event

Notes

Outcome

Uses

Purchased at: _________________________________   Price: _______________

Plant Name	**Date Planted**

Water Requirements   💧   💧💧   💧💧💧   Sunlight

☐ Seed   ☐ Transplant

Date	Event

Notes

Outcome

Uses

Purchased at: ________________________________ Price: ____________